Artful Illusions

Designs to Fool Your Eyes

Aki Nurosi

with Mark Shulman

Sterling Publishing Co., Inc.

New York

To the memory of my father **A.M. Kafi**

Library of Congress Cataloging-in-Publication Available

10 9 8 7 6 5 4 3 2 1

Published in paperback in 2005 by Sterling Publishing Co., Inc.

387 Park Avenue South, New York, NY 10016

Copyright © 2004 Aki Nurosi & Mark Shulman

Concept and design by Aki Nurosi

Text by Mark Shulman and Aki Nurosi

Distributed in Canada by Sterling Publishing

c/o Canadian Manda Group,165 Dufferin Street,

Toronto, Ontario, Canada M6K 3H6

Distributed in Great Britain and Europe by Chris Lloyd at Orca Book

Services, Stanley House, Fleets Lane, Poole BH15 3AJ, England

Distributed in Australia by Capricorn Link (Australia) Pty. Ltd.

P.O. Box 704, Windsor, NSW 2756, Australia

Printed in China

Sterling ISBN 1-4027-1142-5 Hardcover

ISBN 1-4027-2762-3 Paperback

For information about custom editions, special sales, premium and corporate purchases, please contact Sterling Special Sales Department at 800-805-5489 or specialsales@sterlingpub.com.

Acknowledgments

My sincere thanks to Hammett for being so generous in every way, my family, my teachers, my students, Brian Lucid and Ian Clyde for me with the production, and Mark whom I can't thank enough for all that he has done.

—**Aki Nurosi**

For Kara, whose love and support are no illusion. And thanks to Aki for everything I've learned in this process.

—**Mark Shulman**

Contents

You're walking upstairs.

You step onto the dark blue bottom step and begin to climb. Halfway up, you look down and realize the steps are no longer beneath you. They're over your head. There's air below you, and you're falling fast! This can't be real. It has to be an illusion, **and it is**.

Do you get the picture?

You've been climbing Schroeder's Staircase. And you've just descended into the artful world of optical illusions. How did this happen?

There are geometry books and other science books which describe how optical illusions fool the eye. But the basic ideas don't have to be homework.

Your brain naturally tries to see the big picture.

Your brain tries to fit any puzzle pieces into the big picture.

Your brain wants your eyes to make sense of what they see.

Your brain tries to make even impossible things make sense.

Your brain likes to see the impossible, so you get this book.

In a broad sense, if you see something which looks different from its actual measurements, it's an optical illusion.

Illusions use contrast: A shirt with up-and-down stripes can make you look taller and thinner.

Illusions use motion: Circles within circles within circles make you feel like you're falling. And even if you know the pictures in the book are on flat paper, ancient rules of perspective and color help you imagine some are 3-D. We all accept those rules, but they can be broken, and that's how you find yourself on a flipping staircase.

Artful means tricky

The illusions in this book are crafty, and they're art, too. Some may be familiar to you. All of them are designed to open your eyes to the different kinds of illusions you can encounter.

Looking at illusions may take time. Look, and then look again. Watch your first impressions change. And don't worry if you don't see the trick. We all see things differently, and your mind may refuse to be fooled. As you move through the pages, you'll learn which types of tricks affect you most. Then put down the book and look into the real world. They're out there, too.

You'll see.

CAUTION
ILLUSIONS
AHEAD

It all begins with the sun

The sun brings light, and light brings color. Focus on the orange dot in the center of the sun. Does the haze at the sun's edge change color? Now focus on the edge... if you can •

THE SUNFLOWER IS A SUN FOLLOWER, TOO.

Now take your finger and
follow the gray lines.
How many do you see?
Are they all the same color?
Are you sure?
Does any ring seem to be
coming closer?

Take these circles for a spin!

These two circles are the same, except the blue and black are switched.

Try these experiments with one circle, then another.

Keep your eyes on an orange dot and ask yourself:

Are the dark blue bands blending into the light blue background?

Do the gray rings seem to move in the same direction?

What do you see first, rings or rays?

Are both circles the same size?

Think outside the box!

Think straight.

Think the box is straight?

First **use** your eyes,

then **use** a ruler.

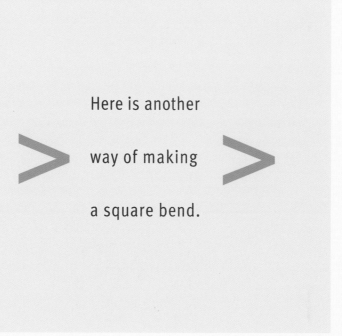

Here is another

way of making

a square bend.

Which Way To Go From Here?

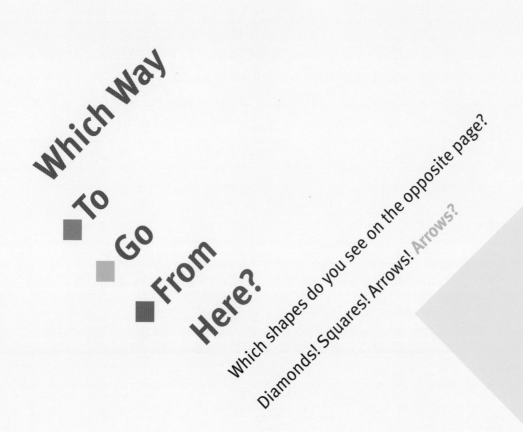

Which shapes do you see on the opposite page?

Diamonds! Squares! Arrows! Arrows?

HOLD ON

TO YOUR

HATS

Are these hats:

a. Taller than they are wide? **b.** Wider than they are tall? **c.** The same size as each other?

The Stare Way

Put your foot down on the bottom step.

What color is it?

Wait!

What about

these steps?

You are going

in circles **&** going

in squares!

We will never

get anywhere

this way.

Don't look down! You'll get dizzy in the dark!

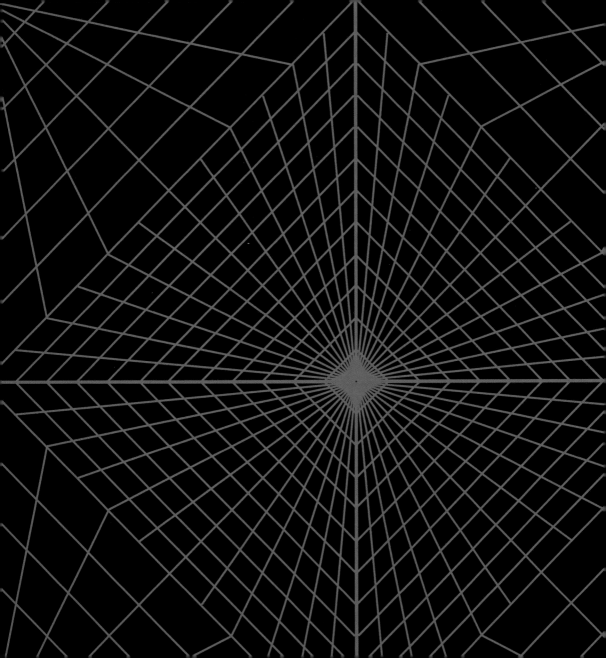

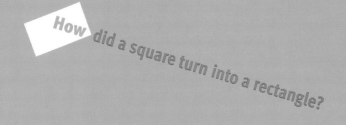

How did a square turn into a rectangle?

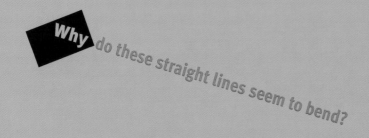

Why do these straight lines seem to bend?

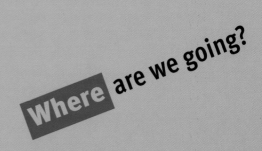

Where are we going?

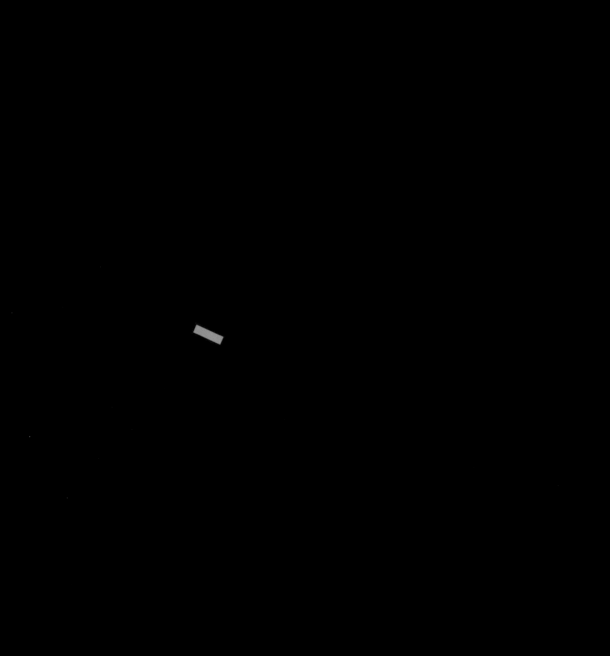

Where did we go?

Try to  in the dark.

You know they are the same.

Turn on the flashlight.

Why do they look so different?

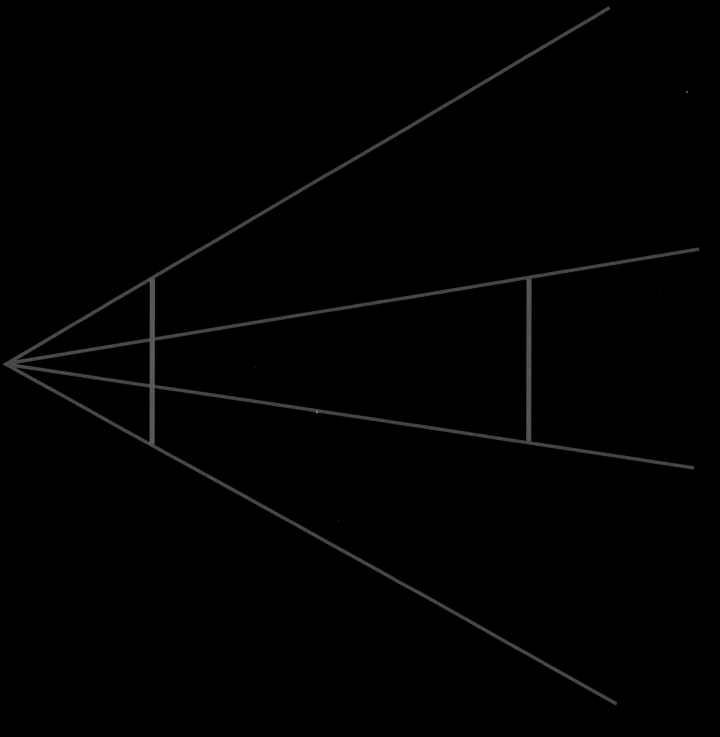

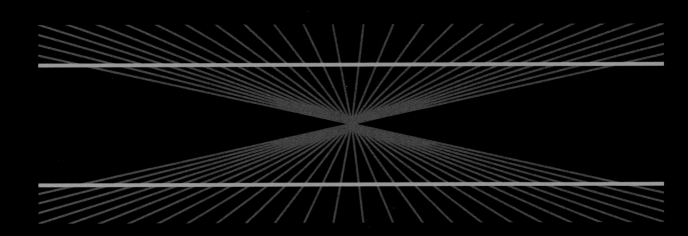

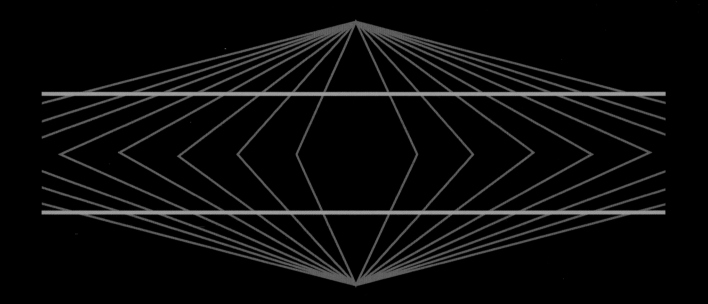

Now let's get something straight around here.

Still in the dark?

Try climbing one of these ladder towers out.

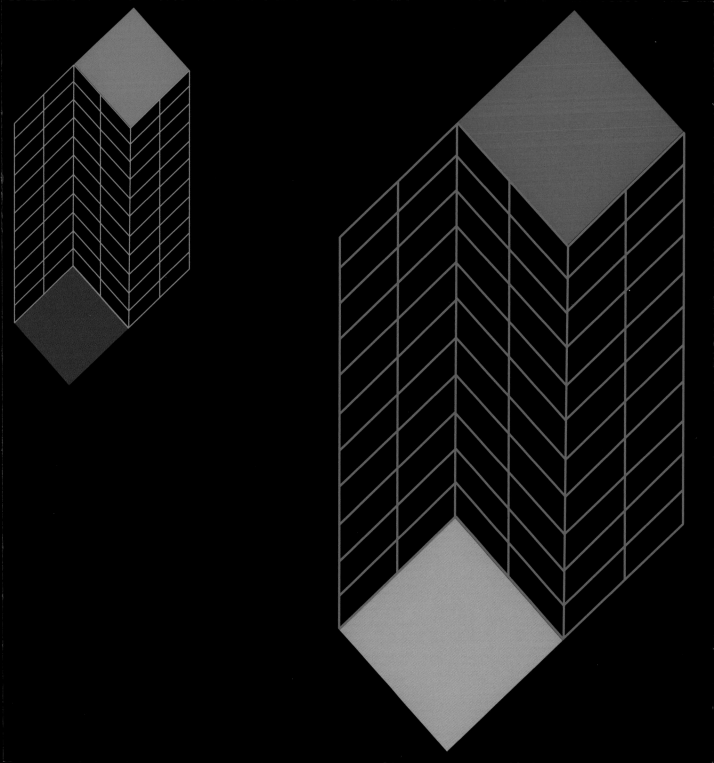

Back to the light.

Anyone can see spots

before their eyes.

Try seeing a square!

Stare at the blue dot in the center

long enough and you'll see some

of the dots change color or even

vanish right in front of your eyes.

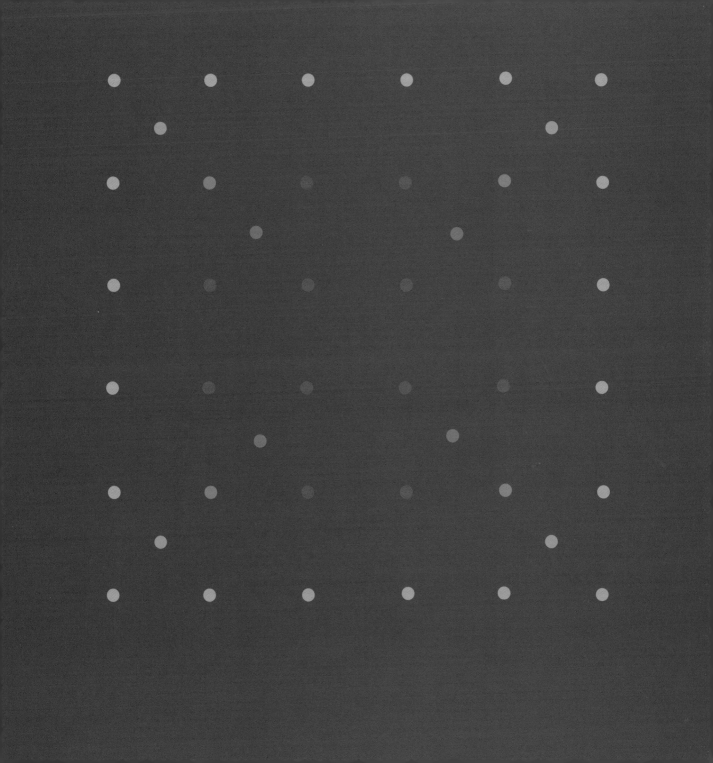

If you put anything

in this box,

it'll probably fall out.

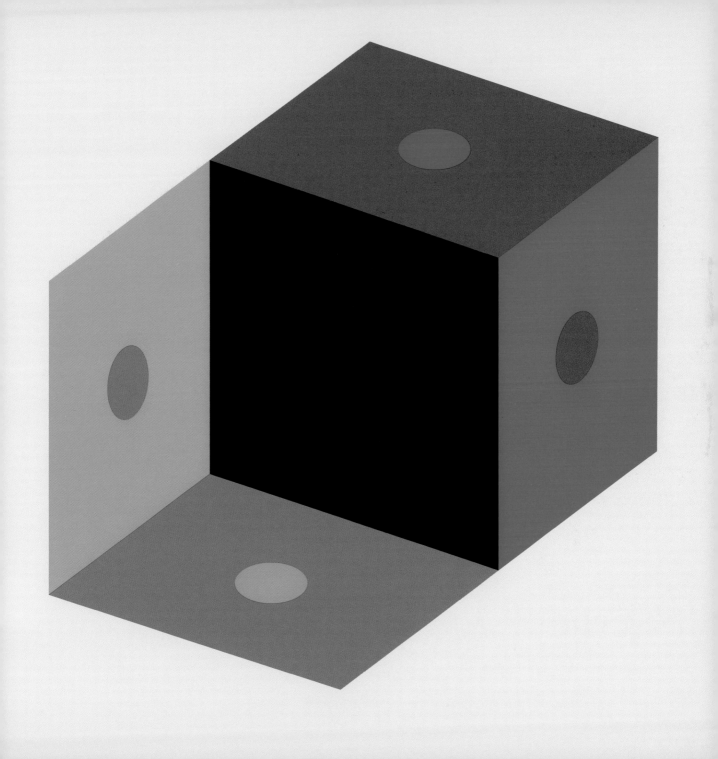

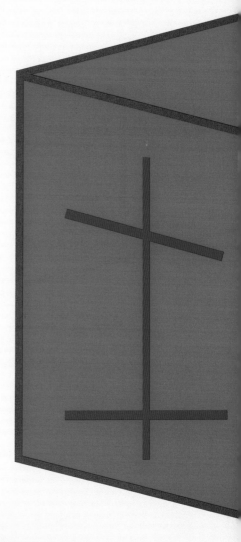

Three dimensions. **Four** intersections. **Two** sets of right angles.

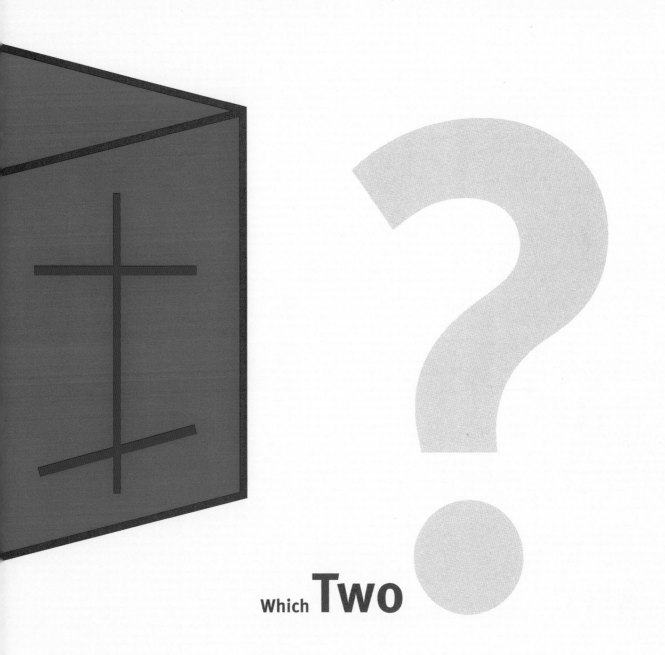

Which **Two**?

The red lines lie parallel.

These boxes rock.

The red boxes lie parallel.

Why do your eyes lie?

Where have all the OC•
TA•
GON?!

Pick a color
and follow
it around all
eight sides.
Around and
around and ...

If you know your **ABCs**
and your **123s,**

then do you know if line $\overline{AB}$ is longer,

shorter, or the same as line $\overline{BC}$ on

figure 1? On figure 2? On figure 3?

Think you know your colors, too?

Are all the **orange** lines the

same on each figure?

What about the other lines?

How can you be so sure?

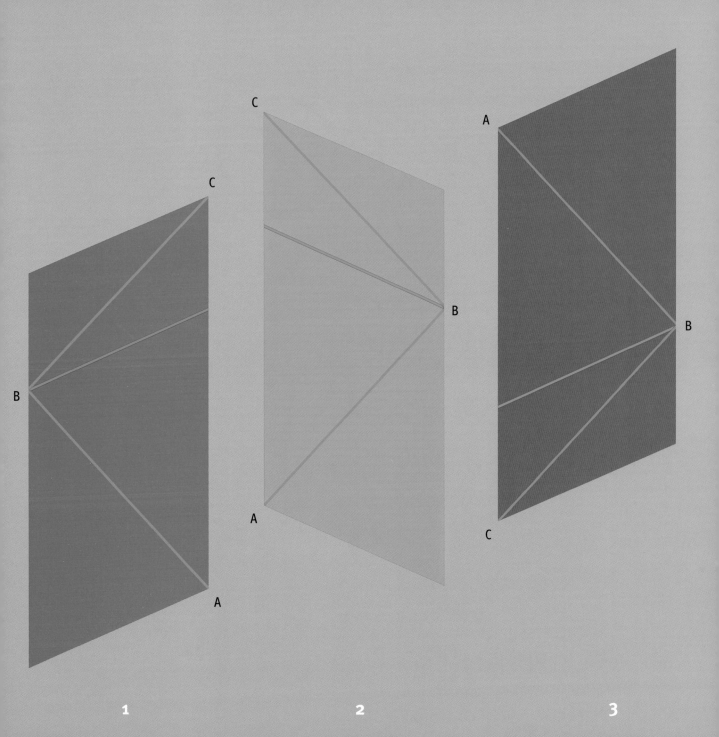

1

2

3

One
line
stops
for
the
red.

The
other
runs
through.

Help
the
stopped
line
catch
up.

Will
it
go
over
or
under
the
finished
line?

⬤ Collecting Box Tops

Where is the ring? Is it on the top of the box? Or the side? Or the bottom?

Or all of the above?

Is it in the front? Is it in the back? Is it suspended in the middle?

Or all of the above?

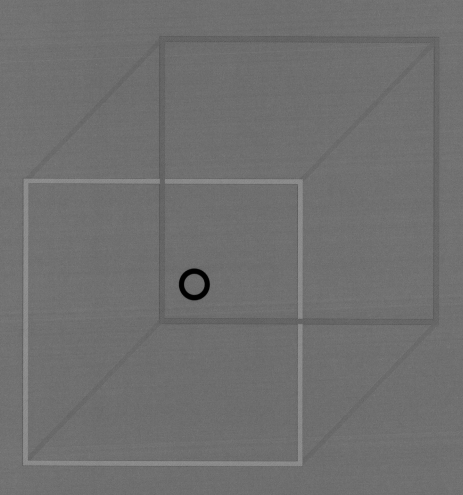

Just blink and re-think!

And while we're at it, are the circles
the same size?

How many triangles? How many squares?
How many septagrams?

Speaking of similar objects that don't look similar,

Maybe.

are the circles the same size? Of course they are.

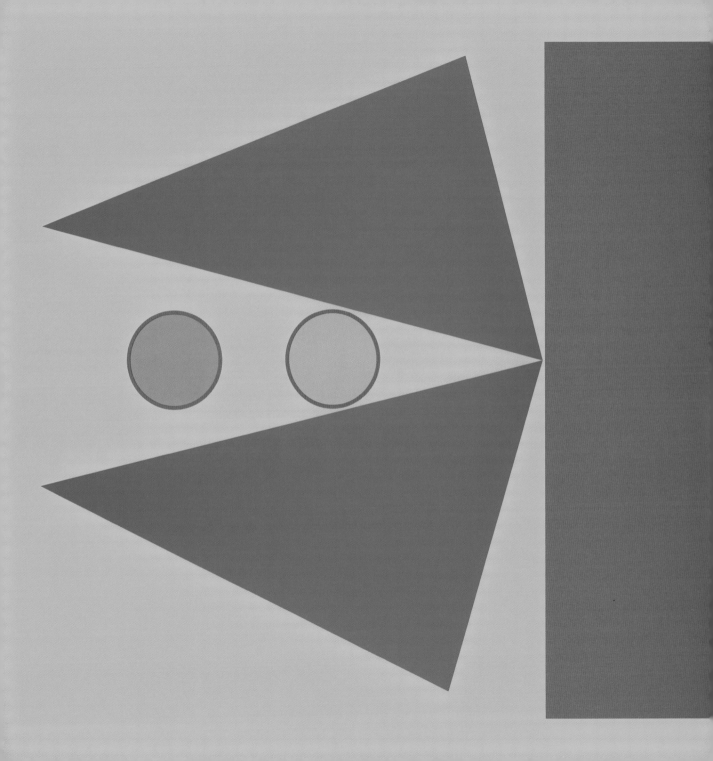

Here's
another
defective
perspective.
What

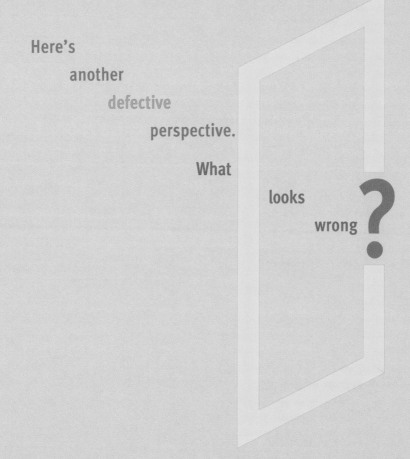

looks
wrong

?

At morning time the sun shines bright.

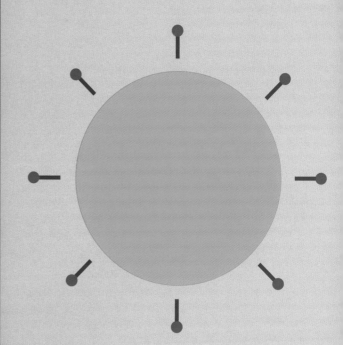

But does the sun shrink down at night?

Illusions Illustrated

Shape Distortions

Location & Direction Distortions

The optical illusions in this book fall under five general types of geometrical illusions.

As you know, in geometry we use shapes that are made of points; lines; planes such as squares, rectangles, triangles and circles; and volumes such as cubes.

Look for the key at the end of each solution to find which type of illusion you're looking at. Here's how each kind of illusion was created.

Place a geometric shape, such as a square or a rectangle, over a field of lines. You'll notice that at certain points, where the geometric shape and the field of lines intersect, the shape appears distorted.

Pages 17, 19, 36–37

Illusions of location and direction are quite striking when encountered. In illusions of location, the actual location of lines and figures is shifted in space although the orientation or inclination of lines remains unaffected. As for illusions of direction, they involve distortions in which the direction or orientation of a contour or figure is altered.

Begin with a bold, solid shape, such as a rectangle. Then add a thinner shape, like a line or an outlined square, within it.

Now change the direction of just the solid shape (rectangle) by tilting it. The outlined square appears to have moved as well.

Also, when the thin line crosses under the bold shape, the thin line appears to shift direction on the way through.

Pages 46–47, 49, 55

Size Distortions

There are a few ways to make objects appear larger or smaller than they really are.
You can compare a vertical line with a horizontal line of the same length.
You can place equal size vertical lines within contrasting angles.
And if you put certain shapes nearer to or further from an object, it will seem to change size.

Reversing Figures

With 3-D illustrations, visual cues help you recognize what you're looking at, like the "top" of a box, or the "bottom" of stairs.
If you give a geometric figure, such as a line or a square, two sets of contradictory visual clues, the figure tends to reverse its position in space as your attention shifts from one set of cues to the other.

Other Distortions

Your eyes get tricked by all kinds of unexpected visual twists and turns. Different types of clever illusions will let you experience motion, depth, unlikely structures, camouflaged or invisible forms, disappearance of certain shapes or colors, and the emergence of other forms.
And that's just the beginning.
Have fun!

Pulsating Sun

When you stare long enough at one color, that color disappears and its opposite color actually appears. That's

called an afterimage. • And what's the opposite of red? Chances are, you saw green along the hazy edges. • As with the real sun, you can't really focus on the edges of this one, either. That's because the green and red work against each other to create a vibrating effect. • As an added bonus, move the book back and forth at arms' length while keeping your eyes fixed at the orange dot.

(Other Distortion) **Page 11**

Ring of Flowers

How many gray rings are on the page? There are two. One is in the yellow, and the other runs around the far outside.

But wait, you say, what about the one in the middle? Aha, we say, it's not a ring. It's just the blue line taking a break. • When spaces and areas are defined by what's around them, we can't help but combine those areas into shapes.

(Other Distortion) **Page 13**

Spinwheels

When you look directly at the orange dot, you lock your eyes in one place. This lets the colors and shapes create

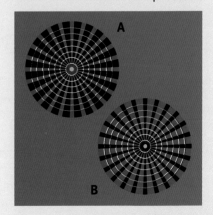

illusions at the outer edge. • While you focus, the blue background helps the blue in circle **A** fade from sight. So, the black rays get all your attention. • The white circles near the center gradually turn dark gray. Your eye naturally follows this transition—that's the pulsating motion you're sensing in the rings. • The circles are both the same size, but you may feel that the blacker (denser) circle **A** is bigger.

(Other Distortion) **Page 15**

Orbison's Illusion

Your brain wants all the circles to make sense together, so it convinces you that you're seeing either a tunnel

going down, or a mountain coming up. Either way, there's the illusion of depth. ■ Now put the square over this tunnel or mountain. The straight lines start bending as if the 3-D shape were actually affecting it.

(Shape Distortion) **Page 17**

Hering's Variant

If a line-up of circles can seem deep, why can't diagonal lines? Stare at them long enough and they appear to

move. ■ Once they start moving for you, the borders of the square start curving. Most people see the square curve in on the right and out on the left.

(Shape Distortion) **Page 19**

Point Counterpoint

Anyone can see squares and diamonds. But some people can never find the arrows without help.

If you can find them, you're golden. And so are the arrows. The boxes hide the arrows, and the arrows hide the boxes, depending on your point of view. Once you convince your eyes to turn the purple boxes into negative space, you'll be positively amazed. ■ Furthermore, the totally balanced (symmetrical) design makes it hard to see anything else but the shapes in the brightest color.

(Other Distortion) **Page 21**

As you probably guessed, the hats are as wide as they are long. So why do they look so tall?

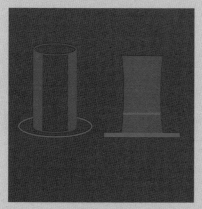

Because we tend to overestimate vertical measurements. Chances are, you're more impressed by a standing tree than a fallen tree that's even longer.

(Size Distortion) **Page 23**

Since your eye is drawn to the red first, you most likely saw a red wall on the staircase. In that case, the

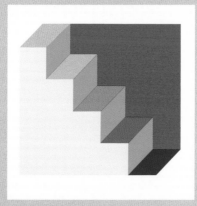

lowest step is orange. Now move your eyes to the purple wall. Suddenly the stairs are moving in a completely different direction and the bottom step is now dark blue. If you hold the book upside-down you will find your bottom step is purple. It's a good first step.

(Reversing Figure) **Page 25**

Here's another stairway to keep you staring. What's the official term for illusions like this?

Impossible object. How does a 3-D object become impossible? Simple— it's not 3-D. It's a 2-D piece of paper, remember? You can do a lot in 2-D, especially when it pretends to have depth. But it's still just a piece of paper.

(Other Distortion) **Page 27**

Welcome to the dark side. How does this illusion take you down, down, down? The lines at the corners get

narrower and narrower—the same trick of perspective used by artists to make lines vanish naturally in the distance. ▪ Once you're convinced the outer corners are "level ground," then the square in the center must be a deep hole. You fell for it.

(Other Distortion) **Page 29**

How did a square turn into a rectangle? Very slowly. That's how. Each inner box evolved a little longer and a

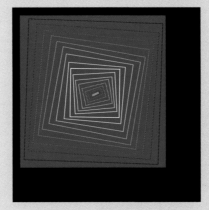

little thinner than the one before. But you can hardly notice from one box to the next. The back-and-forth twirling effect also helps hide the extra space caused by the changes. ▪ The lines seem to bend because your brain tries to line up the tunnel of boxes evenly. By filling in the uneven gap between the uneven boxes, your brain makes the lines bend a little.

(Other Distortion) **Page 31**

The Ponzo illusion is a tried-and-true scheme to scam your eyes. The red doors may be the same length, and

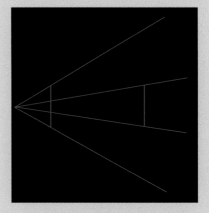

you may know it, but the angled lines seem to stretch the door on the left, and shrink the door on the right. Another trick of perspective.

(Size Distortion) **Page 35**

Hering's Illusion

The pink lines stretch wide, aiming north and south. Your mind tries to make the straight orange lines follow

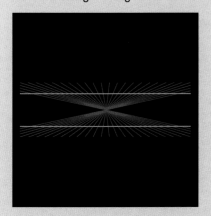

along, and so they seem to bend away from each other. But things are not how they seem.

(Shape Distortion) **Page 36**

Wundt's Illusion

Hering made the straight orange lines bend outward, but Wundt won't. The blue lines in the "diamonds" point

outward, and they seem to pull the orange lines along with them. The result? Straight lines that appear to bend toward each other.

(Shape Distortion) **Page 37**

Thiery's Illusion

The ladder towers seem to be 3-D. The towers that climb up towards the light are sharing a wall with the ladders

that climb down toward a different light. ◆ Because the parallel lines in the middle are tilting, they seem to be (impossibly) in two different dimensions at the same time.

(Reversing Figure) **Page 39**

Bright, Dark, and Square

See the square? Look closely and where you see straight-sided semi-circles you'll find the illusion of a

complete square. Your brain naturally creates shapes and figures where there are loosely defined spaces. And when you find the square, you will also notice that it's darker than the area around it. Why? Because when a shape seems to be placed over other figures it tends to appear a different shade.

(Other Distortions) **Page 41**

Blind Spots

Believe it or not, we all have blind spots. This illusion can show you what you can't see.

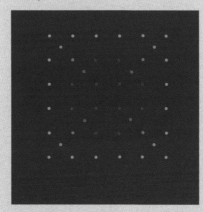

Stare at the blue dot in the middle and keep your focus there. •The red dots disappear because they fall on the portion of your eye's retina which doesn't see. You see?

(Other Distortion) **Page 43**

The Beaunis Cube

But when is a cube not a cube? When it's really two cubes sharing the same center. ▪The black becomes

part of the orange & blue cube, and then part of the red & gray one, almost at the same time. It's another 3-D illusion which is really 2-D. The illusion is simple, but your reaction is not.

(Reversing Figure) **Page 45**

Each of the green vertical lines is crossed with two horizontal lines. One line makes perfect right angles,

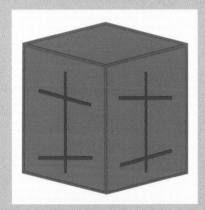

the other does not. With the angled sides of the cube, it's hard to tell which angle's right. ▪ On the left side, the bottom intersection makes right angles. On the right side, it's the top intersection. All right?

(Location/Direction Distortion)

Page 46–47

What's on the outside can affect what's on the inside. ▪ Our eye is drawn to the stronger images—the frames—so

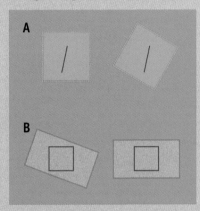

whatever happens to them seems to happen to the weaker red lines inside, too. The parallel red lines haven't moved, but the tilted orange box makes them look as if they have.

(Location/Direction Distortion)

Page 49

Here's an illusion without a conclusion. Where one side should meet another, the surfaces are switched and go off in

the wrong direction. These eight sides will never agree.

(Other Distortion) Page 51

The Sander Parallelogram

All the orange lines are the same length, though line $\overline{AB}$ probably seems a lot longer. That's the angled perspective of

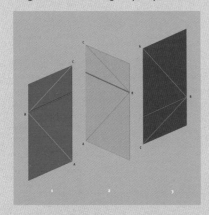

the colored rectangles playing tricks with your eyes. ▪ All the orange lines are the same color, too. When they're placed on the different color backgrounds, the contrast effect makes the lines seem to change color. ▪ If the other lines look different, that's because they actually are different. Surprise.

(Size Distortion) **Page 53**

Poggendorff's Illusion

The red post makes it hard to say which line keeps going, and which one is stopped. If you haven't guessed already,

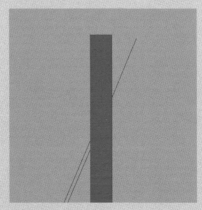

here's your last chance. The shorter line is the upper line. Only the lower line is continued on the right side.

(Location/Direction Distortion)

Page 55

The Necker's Cube

A cube is a cube, no matter how you look at it. Right? But where in the cube is that ring? ▪ You can find it

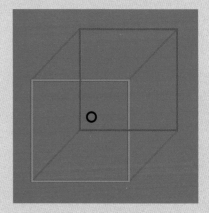

on the top, on the side, on the bottom, and in the middle—you can see it anywhere—and neither you nor the cube ever have to move.

(Reversing Figure) **Page 57**

The circle in the middle probably seems like it's closer to you, since it's placed on top of the triangle shape

(which is blocking all the other shapes). Closer objects tend to appear brighter and smaller. The identical circle on the right looks further away, and so it appears bigger. ▪ Now about those triangles: What's the only rule for a triangle? Do any of these shapes follow that rule? ▪ No, no four-sided squares, either. ▪ But there is one red septagram (seven-sided shape). And you thought this one would be easy?

(Size Distortion) **Page 59**

No matter which angle you choose, placing something (the circle on the right) close to an angle can make it

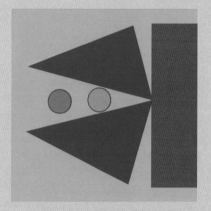

look bigger than its far-away twin (the circle on the left).

(Size Distortion) **Page 61**

Fake 3-D lets you have even faker dimensions. The open rectangle should fit naturally into the solid one, but the

inside wall is lining up with the outside wall on the top left which can't be, oh well, never mind. It's just fun to look at. It's an illusion!

(Other Distortion) **Page 63**

Rays In, Rays Out

When the sun's rays go inside-out at night, the sun looks smaller, too. Having rays that point out makes

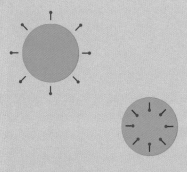

the first circle (top left) look bigger.

(Size Distortion)

Pages 64–65

Farewell

Congratulations!

After a journey like this, you may find that what looks real isn't, and what looks false isn't either.

Glossary

Contradictory
When things are compared, and cannot be both true, they are contradictory.

Distortion
What happens when something's shape is changed, or when it has become misleading.

Figure
In this book, a figure is a drawing which represents a complete shape or group of shapes.

Impossible Object
A figure designed in such a way that it could not possibly exist in the real world.

Negative Space
The area within a shape or group of shapes which only exists because of the shapes which surround it. The hole in a donut is a negative space.

Perception
As a verb, it's using your senses to gather information about something. As a noun, it's the conclusion you reach after gathering the information.

Perspective
How objects appear, depending on where you are as you look at them. When you stand at the bottom of a skyscraper, your perspective makes it seem wide at the bottom and thinner at the top. If you change your position, your perspective changes.

Pulsating
Appearing to expand and contract, or to vibrate.

Symmetrical
When something appears balanced or identical on either side of its center point.

Index

The End